The Enchanted Valley

A Guide to the Myths and Legends of the Llanthony Valley

By M.E. Warren

First published March 2020

EAN 978-1-9164731-0-2

Text and Images © Copyright Melanie Warren 2020

Foliate Head Press
22 Charles Street, Lancaster
LA1 4UU UK

info@foliatehead.com
www.foliatehead.com

Cover Design: Sophie Page

Printed by Book Printing UK
Remus House, Coltsfoot Drive, Peterborough, PE2 9BF

Acknowledgements

For Kate, Georgia and Keeva, Owen and Jemma, Penny, all the friends who have accompanied us to Castle Farm over the years, and finally for Uncle Jim, whose considered opinion on the extraordinary beauty of the place was, 'This really is an enchanted valley, isn't it?' Thank you for the title, Uncle Jim.

Thanks are also due to Carol Watkins for her care and attention over the years, and to James and Thekla March-Smith, without whom Castle Farm would not have become our second home.

www.capel-y-ffin.co.uk

Foreword

Crammed with beauty and mystery, *The Enchanted Valley* is a love letter to the Llanthony valley as it delves into the history and stories behind a landscape and its community. Warren writes with the wonder and intrigue of a visitor to the valley, yet with an intricate knowledge and love that only one who knows a place intimately can have.

While the Llanthony Valley appears as a place where an old-world idyll still reigns, Warren breaks apart the verdant grasses to unleash the history seeping from every dry stone wall, each timber post. This is the landscape where panoramas from *An American Werewolf in London* were filmed, a land where witch-queens were in league with the Devil and the restless dead lurk in the darkness. After reading these collected tales of folk magic, of the roads where Crusaders walked, the Llanthony Valley will never be quite the same again. You'll be watching over your shoulder on each sunlit walk, taking care that the Old Lady of the Mountains isn't leading you astray. From water-horses, corpse candles and women who shape-shift into hares, to rag trees and saintly apparitions, this is a place of fairies and miracles.

A fantastically readable journey through an incredible landscape, *The Enchanted Valley* is a compelling companion to any traveller walking this ancient landscape, wishing to uncover its timelessness and beauty. This is certainly a book you can't put down!

Dee Dee Chainey
Author of *A Treasury of British Folklore* National Trust 2018

The Enchanted Valley

Contents

Introduction

For ten years, our family and assorted friends have spent time in the Llanthony Valley. From the delightful village of Hay-on-Wye, one ascends the hillside along Forest Road, before taking a right turn towards Capel y Ffin. Then the road crosses swathes of moorland at a height which offers a breath-taking view over a patchwork landscape. This is, in fact, the highest road in all of Wales. Finally passing between the peaks of Hay Bluff and Lord Hereford's Knob, one enters the secluded Llanthony Valley, which stretches from this point all the way to Abergavenny, some twenty miles distant. Driving along the only road through the valley is a joy; the landscape never disappoints and each bend in the road presents a fresh combination of fields, mountains, wilderness and trees to satisfy the eye.

But to experience the Llanthony Valley properly, one must leave the car and explore, seek out those old places where a sense of timelessness tugs at the heart. For my family and I, our first hint of this came at our own holiday venue, Castle Farm near Capel y Ffin, where the oldest part of the farmhouse is dug into the hillside to provide shelter against inclement weather. The depth of the windowsills shows the thickness of these walls which must have stood here for three centuries or more, and the stonework of the huge fireplace still bears the marks where metal bars and hooks once suspended cooking pots over the flames. The bookcase in the living room was once the main doorway into the farmhouse, a realisation which makes it easy for a dreamer beside the log fire to imagine how a family might have lived when the building was new.

Behind the farmhouse is an ancient barn whose perfectly straight walls were built without a trace of mortar and whose roof is supported by whole tree trunks. The same men responsible for the barn surely also built the nearby dry-stone walls with their step-stiles allowing easy access to the mountainside. These were not modern workmen, for sure - the admirable skills illustrated here are all but forgotten, now.

Besides Castle Farm, however, there are many other places in this valley where the centuries seem to have paused in their relentless progress to modernity.

The 12th century archdeacon Giraldus Cambrensis (Gerald of Wales) wrote copiously about his travels through Wales and describes the Llanthony Valley, 'which is shut in on all sides by a circle of lofty mountains and which is no more than three arrow-shots in width...' Twenty miles in length, the Llanthony Valley is one of the loveliest in Wales and although it is largely uninhabited, there is something about the atmosphere of the place which has drawn artists, writers and other dreamers to settle here, inspired by the landscape and the peace to produce some of their finest work. Among the list are names such as Bruce Chatwin, Eric Ravilious, Eric Gill, Walter Savage Landor, Raymond Williams and Allen Ginsburg.

The road which passes through the valley is known as Gospel Pass, said to be named after the 12th century Christian soldiers who travelled through the area, raising funds for the Third Crusade. Whatever the truth of that supposition, Gospel Pass is an entirely appropriate name for the single-track road which meanders through this lovely valley, leading us from one ancient church to the next.

The 18th century church at Capel-y-Ffin, dedicated to St. Mary the Virgin, stands on the site of a much older building. Behind the church is a Baptist chapel, converted from a 17th century house and perhaps the oldest Baptist chapel in existence.

Close by are the ruins of a Benedictine monastery; established in 1869, it fell into private hands in the 1920s and for several years was home to a succession of artists and writers. Only a few miles farther on is Llanthony Priory, a glorious ruin, and St. David's Church, built on the site of St. David's original monastic cell. St. Martin's Church at Cwmyoy dates from the 13th century and is known for its crooked interior and the 14th century roadside cross it houses. At Patrishow there is a wonderfully ancient church boasting medieval wall-paintings and a sacred well.

This book will introduce you to all these places and more besides, including the folklore and myths associated with them. It should come as no surprise that the landscape of the Llanthony Valley is home to fairies, that the oldest buildings harbour ghosts, or that holy wells have miracle stories attached to them. Special attention is also paid to Father Ignatius, the founder of Llanthony Tertia monastery at Capel y Ffin, who was credited with several miracles here. In this magical place, those miracles are easy to believe.

It has been a delight to research these stories and present them in this book. To you, my reader, I wish you the same joy I felt when discovering these places and these tales for the first time.

Melanie Warren, 2020

Francis Kilvert

A wonderful source of information about the area from Hay to Abergavenny can be found in the diaries of Francis Kilvert, a country curate who served in the area from 1865 - 1872. Kilvert was curate at St. Michael's Church in Clyro, close to Hay-on-Wye. He lived at Ashbrook House and his diary makes it clear that he spent most of his days out and about, visiting parishioners and making friends with all manner of people, far and wide.

Kilvert wrote copiously about the landscape, the people, the characters he met. He had a fondness for elderly people who could regale him with tales of ghosts and superstition, stories they had heard from their grandmothers, stories that reached back through the centuries to the ancient mythology which is ever-present in the Welsh landscape.

It is clear from Kilvert's diary that the old beliefs and superstitions were not just distant memories; even in the late 19th century, his parishioners still used traditional methods to help them in times of need. On one occasion a woman left her washing out overnight on the hedge by the church and came to it next morning to find some underclothes missing. Determined to find the thief and retrieve her property, she and her husband consulted the commonly used divinatory tools of a Bible and a key. There were two methods of combining these items for use as an oracle; in the first, the key was inserted into the Bible and held gently in the hands whilst the names of the suspects were spoken aloud. Eventually the key would move, seemingly of its own accord. The second method involved placing the key in the Bible which was then suspended until it began to sway or revolve at mention of the guilty party. Whichever method was used, the name which apparently triggered the movement was confidently claimed to be that of the perpetrator.

One can accept the use of the Bible as a divining tool in those days, as it was still regarded by most as a holy and spiritual book, containing the word of God himself. However, in the case mentioned by Kilvert, the woman's husband double-checked the result by using an older, more grisly, ritual. He incarcerated a toad inside a ball of clay, with a piece of paper. The clay parcel was then baked in the fire. Once 'cooked', the parcel would be broken open in the belief that the toad, in his distress, would have scratched the guilty person's name on the paper! Kilvert does not tell us if the latter method worked...

Also at Clyro, where Kilvert lived, is the Baskerville Hall Hotel. In Kilvert's day this was the family home of Thomas Mynors Baskerville, a surname which is familiar from Arthur Conan Doyle's novel featuring a terrifying otherworldly hound. In fact, the Baskerville family really did have a connection with fierce dogs, although this was more properly associated with a different branch of the family who lived in Oxfordshire, at Crowsley Park House. Crowsley was once owned by Sir Henry Baskerville and its gateposts were topped with statues of what could only be described as 'hellhounds'. Another statue adorned the lintel of the main door. One of Doyle's friends, James Molloy, married Sir Henry's daughter, Florence. It is surely no coincidence that Conan Doyle named one of his main characters after Sir Henry.

It is said that the Hall in Conan Doyle's famous novel is based on Baskerville Hall, although many other grand Halls claim this honour and, of course, Crowsley Park is a strong contender. However, Conan Doyle was certainly associated with the Baskervilles and is said to have visited Clyro many times, so his presence is quite rightly reflected in the décor of many of the rooms here.

Baskerville Hall Hotel is set in over a hundred acres of countryside overlooking the River Wye. The gardens are haunted by a 'white lady' and, inside the house, a ghostly man has often been seen on the main staircase, where footsteps have also been heard. Their connections to the Hall are unknown.

The hound featured in Conan-Doyle's novel about the Baskervilles never really existed, of course - or did it? And does it still? In 1989 the Independent newspaper featured a story about dozens of sheep in the area which had been horribly mutilated, allegedly by a 'dog-like animal'. The urge to suggest that the animal might have been a descendant of the Baskervilles' own hounds must have been irresistible and I think the journalist can be forgiven for mentioning it. However, a story from a decade later is a little more worrying...

A chef at the Baskerville Hall Hotel was working alongside three colleagues when he suddenly cried out in pain. His colleagues asked what was the matter and he told them that he had seen the shadowy figure of a dog in the kitchen with them and then felt a sharp nip on his thigh. Naturally, his colleagues did not take him seriously, as they had seen nothing themselves, but by the next day a nasty bruise mark had appeared on his leg...

Hay-on-Wye

The delightful village of Hay-on-Wye is largely made up of early 19th century buildings with older ones here and there. It lies at the foot of the hill which bears Hay Castle, parts of which date from the 13th century. The oldest building, apart from the Castle itself, is surely the Chapel of St. John, on Lion Street. It was founded in 1254 and was used by Hay's Guild of Tradesmen, as well as serving as the Castle's chapel.

Hay-on-Wye's main attraction is the number of bookshops it holds. There are around twenty; some specialise in one genre such as children's books, or crime fiction, but most offer an unending variety of titles in an array of genres. If you love books, it is very easy to lose a day here. It is also almost impossible to lose one's way in the village. When I visit there with friends and family, we have become accustomed to wandering off in various directions, never thinking of arranging to meet up later, because we know by now that we will certainly bump into each other several times during the day.

Francis Kilvert mentions Hay in a diary entry for July 15th, 1870. He visited friends at the Castle for tea and then went to the Swan Hotel to collect 'Miss Lyne and her brother'. These were the siblings of Father Ignatius, who was at that time building his monastery in Capel-y-Ffin.

We will hear much more about Father Ignatius, later.

Francis may have been a clergyman but, as his diary shows, he was also a romantic at heart. His entry for July 15th describes Miss Lyne's beautiful hands and comments that he will be sorry to see her leave next day, just when he is beginning to know her. He finds the news 'provoking'. However, Miss Lyne is only one of the young women he writes about admiringly. Amongst others, he several times describes the many attractions of a young woman working in the sunshine outside Chapel Cottage at Capel y Ffin.

We must not forget that Kilvert was a young man when he lived at Clyro; only twenty-five years old when he arrived in the village in 1865. His diaries are all the more poignant when it is realised that in 1879, this enthusiastic and romantic young man was to die, only five weeks after finally marrying, and at the tragically young age of only thirty-nine.

Hay Castle, where Kilvert had tea that day in 1870, has stood proudly above the village for almost a thousand years. The square keep of the castle is said to have been built around 1200 AD by Maud de Braose, a remarkable woman whose husband William was a favourite companion and ally of King John and about whom several tales are told.

Some of the stories about Maud de Braose refer to her as Matilda, not Maud, and still others give her the nickname of Moll Walbee. In the latter form, the stories are really legends which portray her as a witch or, at the very least, a woman in league with the Devil. The factual stories that history tells about Maud are sometimes blurred by the legends told about Moll Walbee but that is not surprising when one understands how influential and powerful she was.

Maud was born around 1155 AD, in France, daughter to Bernard de St. Valery. Her nickname, Walbee, probably derives from centuries of mispronunciations of her maiden surname. She married William de Braose, who was Lord of several townships from Hay to Abergavenny. He was also made Lord of Limerick when his friend King John was crowned. Maud was, by association, a woman of great power.

Maud understood her lofty position well and when William went to war and left her in charge, she rose to the challenge. in 1198 she defended Painscastle against the Prince of Powys, Gwenwynwyn, for three weeks until English troops came to her aid. Maud also gave her husband sixteen children, many of whom are well-documented in history.

In 1208, William de Braose and King John argued, probably over a debt William owed to the King, although the argument was exacerbated when Maud cast doubt on the cause of the death of one of the King's nephews. When King John heard her accusations he demanded that William's first-born son should be imprisoned in recompense. Maud, quite naturally, refused to surrender her son to the King, so he responded by seizing all her husband's border castles. Maud and her son escaped to Ireland but were soon captured, brought back to England and imprisoned at Corfe Castle, in Dorset, where they both starved.

It is no wonder that Maud has been immortalised in legend. For example, it is said that she built the Castle of Hay in a single night, carrying the stones in her apron. At one point, she stopped to remove a troublesome pebble from her shoe, casting it across the river to Llowes Churchyard, where it can be seen today. The 'pebble' known as Moll Walbee's stone is, in fact, a huge and ancient cross, now preserved inside St. Meilig's Church.

This story is a good example of a common folkloric explanation for the existence of ancient standing stones or crosses, although the Devil is more usually the featured character, carrying stones in his builder's apron and letting them fall as he flies to his destination. Maud's own story is really an indication of just how powerful she was, for in the eyes of those who observed her from afar, there could be no other explanation for her achievements than witchcraft or a liaison with the Devil.

Another tale is told about a monk who surprised Moll Walbee late one night as she worked on her spells and magical workings. The shocked monk embarked on a mission to save Moll's soul, exhorting her to cease this devilish work and turn instead to God. In response, Moll caught hold of the monk and carried him to the River Wye, where she threw him in and left him to drown. It is said that in certain conditions, the watery calls of the drowning man can still be heard.

Maud de Braose continues to inspire storytellers to this day. She features in several novels, including *Lady of Hay*, written by author Barbara Erskine. She is also mentioned in *Here Be Dragons* by Sharon Penman, *To Defy A King* and *The Scarlet Lion* by Elizabeth Chadwick, and Jean Plaidy's novel *The Prince of Darkness*, about King John.

Like so many other buildings in Hay, part of the Castle was once home to a bookshop which, as can be imagined, was atmospheric in the extreme. Sadly, the bookshop was closed a few years ago, but for a very good reason as extensive remedial works were to be carried out on the whole of the building. Some parts of the exterior walls were so decayed that they were in danger of crumbling away altogether, which would have been nothing short of tragic.

The Castle is open for guided tours and walking through the now empty rooms is even more interesting than exploring the old bookshop. One of the most remarkable details is in an upstairs room where a fireplace sports a lintel formed of a block of stone bearing Celtic knotwork. Clearly the original builders had found the stone lying unwanted and decided to put it to good use, not fully realising its importance. At least it has been preserved!

The Castle is a fascinating mix of architectural styles as new towers and wings have been added over the centuries. Various features are dated from the 12th, 13th and 14th centuries and the attached manor house dates from 1660. With the help of the Hay Castle Trust and funding from the National Lottery, the Castle's future is now secure as a centre for culture, arts and education.

Naturally, there are ghost stories attached to Hay Castle. In the old days, servants were quite used to seeing a lady in a corridor which led from the oldest part of the castle; they were told that if they saw her, they were not to worry but simply stand back and allow her to pass. In the early 20th century the family then inhabiting the castle often saw this same lady standing by the fireside in the living-room. They said that she would simply turn around, smile, and vanish.

A more gruesome tale concerns a housekeeper who was stabbed at the foot of a certain staircase. She did not haunt, but when she died, she dropped her bunch of keys and they landed in a pool of her blood. The outline of the keys can, apparently, still be seen.

Elsewhere in Hay, there's a tale about a house which was unoccupied for many years until it was bought by a couple who were unaware of the house's history. One day, the wife walked into the pantry and found a strange woman standing there. The woman turned, looked at her for a moment and then disappeared. Shocked, the wife ran to a neighbour. Only then did she learn that a woman had taken her own life in the house, many years before - a woman who fitted the description of the ghostly woman in the pantry. Now she and her husband understood why the house had lain empty for so long. The house was reverently exorcised and the woman was never seen again.

An older story is told about the toll gate which used to stand on the Black Lion Bridge. The story was related many years ago by an old lady, who said it had happened to her grandfather when he was a young man. He was approaching the toll gate on horseback one night when he heard another horse behind him, travelling at speed. He pulled his own horse over to allow the other to pass and was almost thrown in the process. When he reached the toll gate, he asked the gate-keeper who the dangerous rider might have been. The gate keeper said no-one else had passed that way for hours.

One of the public houses in Hay (not named) features in a very curious tale. A certain man visited the public house after conducting some business at Hay Fair. As he relaxed with his friends, he suddenly saw some drops of liquid on the table before him which seemed to him to be blood. He was seized by a terrible certainty that his wife, at home, was in trouble. He ran home as fast as he could and found that his wife had been attacked by an intruder who was, even then, hiding behind the settle. So incensed was the man that he fell upon the intruder and killed him. Unable to confess his deed, he buried the intruder close by. As the weeks wore on, the ghost of the intruder made life impossible for the couple until they had no alternative but to leave their home and make a life elsewhere. The house itself remained unoccupied for many years.

And what of fairies? They are certainly not absent from the landscape here. In Welsh they are known as the Tylwyth Teg, which translates as 'the beautiful family'. Are fairies simply mythical creatures, with no reality? On the contrary, for if one believes the folkloric stories, fairies are very real in this part of Wales. The stories are few but that stands to reason, as fairies do not often interact with humans. They are sometimes glimpsed by accident, taken unawares, as in the case of 'the beautiful family' seen dancing amongst a glade of foxgloves, in Cusop, close to Hay. These dancing fairies were observed in 1912 which, whilst over a century ago, is more recently than one would have supposed.

Other stories speak of kindly fairies who offer assistance, such as the Tylwyth Teg who lived in a stand of rocks by the river, close to the old railway station. These fairies took pity on the labourers who worked in the fields, particularly at hay-making time; each day, the labourers would find a meal laid out for them on the rocks, complete with cutlery. This happened every day until one labourer stole a fairy knife as proof of this magical event. This deed was unforgiveable. He did return the knife, but too late - the fairies never left a meal on the rocks again. If you wish to see the spot where the fairies lived, the rocks are just where the Dulas Brook joins the River Wye.

Another story tells of a man who never saw fairies, but who did once hear them talking; they were bemoaning the fact that they could make no bread because they had no peel - a flat shovel - for taking the bread from the oven. Feeling sorry for them, the man went home and fashioned a tiny metal peel, which he left in the spot where he had heard the voices. Next day, he found that the fairies had taken the peel and put it to good use, for they had left him a gift of cakes.

There is one last ghost story I must include, although it is set not in Hay but in Llanigon, a nearby hamlet. In St. Einiog's churchyard a gravestone remembers Joseph Arndell, who died in 1768. It is said that he never went to church and so, after his death, it was suspected that his ghost remained in the village. Six clergymen undertook to lay his ghost to rest, but the ghost responded by appearing as an angry bull, scaring most of the clergymen into silence. Only one of the clergymen continued reciting the necessary prayers and he was eventually rewarded by the sight of the bull slowly shrinking until it was the size of a fly. The fly was trapped in a small box and taken to Joseph's old home, where it was dropped into the well. After that, there were no more hauntings.

What a strange tale!

The Seven Wells of Hay-on-Wye

For such a small village, Hay has a remarkable number of wells, several of which are reputed to have healing or other miraculous qualities. Hay's Tourist Information Centre stocks a handy leaflet which can guide the interested around them all and I would add that the 'sensible shoes' approach is recommended!

There are three wells close to St. Mary's Church. Just below the churchyard is Walk Well, where troublesome spirits were sometimes laid to rest. This well is hard to find as it lies at the bottom of a steep slope, right at the edge of the River Wye, where a wharf existed in medieval times.

The Eye Well, close by, was so named because its water would heal eye complaints, as long as the water was collected at dawn. Such water has since been found to be 'chalybeate', that is, containing iron salts, which would indeed be soothing to sore eyes. The well is accessible, with a little difficulty, if one clambers a little way down the riverbank.

The site of St. Mary's Well was once part of the churchyard but is now the garden of a private house. The well can be seen over the hedge. Its water was used for baptisms and a legend says that when the newly built church tower was on fire, the well gave forth a fountain which doused the flames.

Swan's Well, close to the Swan Hotel, issues from an earthen bank close to a neighbouring stream. Those suffering from sprained ankles or wrists could find a cure by immersing the affected part in the water. On Oxford Road, a plaque on the castle wall marks the walled-up site of St. John's Well, whose water was used for baptisms in St. John's Church. Another plaque on Newport Street marks the site of the Town Well.

The Black Lion Well, on Black Lion Green, is connected to St. Keyna, the 25th daughter of Prince Brychan, after whom Brecon is named. St. Keyna refused to be married and travelled far and wide to avoid the many princes who sought her hand and wherever she stayed, a new spring appeared. She charmed the springs so that the first of a newly-married couple to drink the water would 'wear the trousers' in the relationship. Consequently, some brides would carry a small bottle of the water to the altar with them, to ensure a favourable outcome!

This tradition is famously connected to St. Keyne's Well, in Cornwall, and it is said to have happened often in Hay. A local folklorist, C.G. Portman, relates the story of a wedding in the late 18th century where the bride visited the well as soon as the wedding was over, still clad in her wedding dress, but before she could drink from the water she stumbled into a brook and returned to the wedding party 'greatly besmirched and bedraggled'.

Of all the seven wells in Hay, the Black Lion well is my favourite – mostly because of its location next to the very pretty Black Lion Green. A plaque on a boulder proudly announces the site of the well. A set of steps lead down to it; they appear to be in someone's garden but the owner of the house is more than happy for well-seekers to explore.

Following the map provided by the Tourist Office is by far the easiest way to discover all of Hay's seven wells, and in addition you will also discover other treasures, such as the lovely riverside walk depicted below. It is a very pleasant way to explore areas of Hay which usually go unnoticed.

The Black Mountains

The Black Mountains, to the south of Hay, have earned their name because, quite simply, they often appear to be that colour. My family and I noticed this effect, which is simply a trick of the light, when driving back to Capel y Ffin one afternoon. We were approaching the mountain range from a different direction than usual and, despite the fine day and clear skies, the mountains did indeed stand before us black and forbidding. Generally, travelling towards the Black Mountains from Hay, this aspect is not seen because one looks along the range of mountains rather than seeing its full length dominating the horizon.

One leaves Hay on Forest Road, which very soon becomes a narrow lane (with frequent passing places) travelling steadily upwards between high hedges with only glimpses of the surrounding countryside. A signpost points to Craswall or Capel y Ffin; take the latter direction. After a cattle grid, a final stretch of upward climbing leads to the summit where the vista opens out dramatically, revealing stunning views on all sides; to the left, Hay Bluff with Offa's Dyke on its summit and, to the right, a vast swathe of countryside laid out like a patchwork quilt. Straight ahead is the peak of Twmpa, known in English as Lord Hereford's Knob, marking the edge of the Black Mountain range. The moorland here is inhabited only by sheep and fell ponies who are notoriously unconcerned by cars, so it is fortunate that one cannot drive fast along the road towards Twmpa.

This is a single track road with passing places. These lay-bys should not be used for parking, but at the foot of Hay Bluff there is a long-established parking area. It is well worth taking advantage of this and walking towards the edge of the plateau, where the view before you is extraordinary, no matter what the weather. However, a clear day with some clouds is the most beautiful, as the landscape's textures constantly change under the shadows of the passing clouds. Sometimes rain can be seen in the distance, as misty patches blurring the horizon.

There was once a stone circle, known as Pen y Beacon, on this plateau. All that remains is one slim standing stone and a few flat stones almost hidden in the turf, the rest having long since decayed or been taken away to be put to some other useful purpose. The common question - just why such stone circles were built - is easily answered in a place such as this, for does not the vista encourage a sense of reverence?

Throughout the centuries, the Christian church not only discouraged worship at these places but actively encouraged their destruction. Decrees were issued stating that those who knew of their existence and neglected to tear them down were guilty of sacrilege. We should be thankful, then, that so many still remain, even in their incompleteness, as monuments to the places our ancient ancestors found awe-inspiring. When visiting them, we can only agree with their opinions.

The road here is the highest road in all of Wales and the landscape laid out before you seems to roll on forever. As you continue along this road, with untameable moorland on either side, you may recognise the view from the opening scenes of John Landis' classic movie 'An American Werewolf in London'. Although the scenes are set on the Yorkshire moors, the director was looking for somewhere with a full range of weather conditions. And, as local people will assure you, a full range of weather is certainly on offer on the moorland under Hay Bluff. The village of 'East Proctor' featured in the film was actually the nearby village of Crickadarn and the fictional pub, the 'Slaughtered Lamb', was a house there.

Oddly, werewolves do feature in the folklore tales of the Black Mountains area. They are not common elsewhere in the country so it is somewhat coincidental that this particular location was chosen for the above-mentioned film.

There is a tale about a farming family living somewhere in this county, who had peculiarly large, hairy, pointed ears. All seven children in the family had inherited this trait. When the father of the family was left some money by a relative, he decided to quit the hard farming life all his ancestors had known and leave the farm behind. Everyone who knew the family were glad to see them go. They had long believed that the family was descended from a strange race of people who were half-man, half-wolf, and they were afraid of them.

Subsequent families who tried to make the farm work for them knew no success; sheep and cattle did not survive and crops failed, until eventually it became accepted that the wolf-family must have laid a curse on the place. Many a hardy family tried and failed until the fruitless farm was abandoned altogether.

There is also a tale about a young man who fell in love with a girl who was very pretty but had a terrible temper. They married, but he found it hard to keep his young wife happy.

Eventually, when hard times fell upon the couple, the young husband could not even bring enough food into the house and his bad-tempered young wife lost her patience. She swore that she would go out herself and find enough food for them both.

The food she brought back was good meat and she continued to bring it, a steady supply, until her husband began to worry where it was coming from and insisted that she tell him her secret.

His wife agreed to take him with her when she next went foraging - but first made him promise that no matter what happened, he would not call her by name, not even once, during their expedition. The two of them walked in the countryside until at last they came to a place where some lambs had strayed away from their herd. The wife walked slowly towards one of the lambs and muttered some words, though her husband could not tell what they were. Her words must have been some kind of spell for as he watched, she turned into a wolf! In this guise, she quickly grabbed one of the lambs and ran away with it, leaving her husband to return to their home alone.

She came home herself later that evening, once more his pretty young wife, and she brought with her a good supply of meat.

After this, the two of them often went out foraging together, until one evening when his wife turned into a wolf and was chased by a farmer and his dogs. Fearing for her life, the young husband forgot his wife's warning never to use her name and called out, "Come home, Gwenllian, come home!" As soon as the words had been uttered, the wolf disappeared and there was the young wife, lying hurt on the ground.

The farmer, seeing her like that, soon spread the word amongst the local people and forever after that she was known as 'wolf-woman', although her magic had vanished the moment her husband called her name. She and her husband had to pay for their meat from then on.

There may not really be any werewolves in the Black Mountains area, but there is at least one spectre, the Old Lady of the Mountains, who has been seen many times over the centuries. She appears to those walking the mountains, often at night, and those who see her are invariably led astray as they follow her, wanting to ask directions from her or thinking she is in need of help, for what would an old woman be doing, wandering the mountainside all alone? There is one form of protection against being led astray by this ghostly old lady; travellers are advised to first go to Craswall and lay a bowl of water at the foot of the maypole. Quite why this should have the desired effect is not known, although some do say that the old woman is the ghost of a witch who was burned at the stake; the water shows sympathy, at least.

Deep in the Valley

Passing between Twmpa and Hay Bluff, Gospel Pass travels along the side of a mountain, overlooking the valley below and mountains beyond it. Ahead, a range of peaks can be seen, where horses and sheep graze together and mists gather on the summits. Then the road descends, slowly at first and then all the way to the valley floor, into a tunnel of trees that stretches for a mile or more, all the way to Capel y Ffin.

This is a magical stretch of road, winding along as it follows the course of the River Honddu. It is worn down by centuries of travellers who came this way.

Until 1960 this road was unsurfaced and deemed not suitable for motor vehicles; the local postman made his deliveries in this area wholly on foot. His route was fourteen miles long and it took him eight hours to complete.

In some places the fields on either side are several feet above the road itself, which clearly shows the age of this thoroughfare and qualifies it for the term 'holloway'. Passing between the heavy growth of ancient hedges with trees touching each other overhead, particularly when the sun creeps between the leaves and dapples the road ahead, it feels as if one is traversing some kind of fairyland.

Driving along this road is a joy as long as you're in no hurry; you'll be travelling at around 20 miles per hour, no more, with pauses in passing places to make way for oncoming cars. Make mental notes about those passing places for occasions when you're obliged to reverse.

If you have time, it is well worth walking this stretch of road. There is room to leave your car at Capel y Ffin, near the church. It is entirely worth the effort; I have walked this route at dawn and dusk, in all weathers, in summer and in winter. Even though part of me would like to keep this walk a secret, just for my enjoyment alone, I am compelled to recommend it as one of the loveliest walks you will ever take.

Capel Y Ffin

Eventually, the valley road emerges from the overhanging trees and the tiny hamlet of Capel y Ffin is reached. The only landmarks visible from the road are a farmhouse, a chapel, and a red telephone box. Lanes leading off the road to left and right lead to a few other dwellings but at first sight, Capel y Ffin hardly even exists. It comes as no surprise to learn that this isolated little place was the last community in this part of Wales to speak Welsh.

We start with the chapel; the Church of St. Mary the Virgin. Welsh churchyards often contain yew trees, whether the churches are large or small. They may contain a single tree, or a few, but the Church of St. Mary the Virgin is surrounded by them. The church measures only twenty-three feet by fifteen, so the encircling grove is a close planting of trees and it feels like a miniature forest. It is a place of enchantment.

Inside the porch, the noticeboard proudly carries a certificate which states that the trees are at least five centuries old. But as I was looking closely at the yews one morning, a passer-by informed me that they were much older than that - dendrochronology has established that they have been in this tiny place for some fifteen centuries, not merely five. This is easy to believe when one looks again at their size, their girth and their aged appearance.

The real question is why were they planted here? Some claim simply that the thick foliage of the yew offered protection against the elements, especially for early churches, which were simple wooden structures. Others claim that they were planted and nurtured for the making of longbows, for which purpose their wood had perfect qualities. But it is also true that the yew has been venerated by the Welsh throughout history and was often commemorated in the songs and poems of Welsh bards and poets.

There is no doubt that the yew is a sacred tree. In early Christianity yew branches were cast into the grave for the coffin to rest upon, and used to decorate churches on holy occasions. The evergreen nature of its foliage led to the yew being seen as a symbol of immortality. However, the symbolism of the yew is far older than Christianity. It is thought that many Welsh churchyards were built on Druidical sites, their circular shape pointed out as evidence.

With all this in mind and given the age of the yews surrounding St. Mary's, the fact that they stand in a circle and, not least, the peacefulness of the place, it seems obvious that the site of this charming little church was regarded as a sacred place long before Christianity reached the valley.

Francis Kilvert described the little church as looking like a 'stout grey owl' and its porch is certainly beak-like. It was built in 1762 on the site of a previous church, which is believed to have replaced a still earlier one. Despite its small stature it boasts a bell-tower which leans charmingly at an angle. Inside is a medieval octagonal font, possibly brought here from another church elsewhere, but it is just as likely to have belonged to all the churches which have stood in this place. In the churchyard is the shaft and base of a medieval cross.

Two of the graves in the churchyard bear headstones which were carved by the famous sculptor Eric Gill, who lived in the village for many years, residing at the nearby monastery along with his enclave of artist friends. More about him will be found in a later chapter, about Llanthony Tertia Monastery.

Behind St. Mary's Church is the River Honddu and, across the water, a Baptist chapel which is not open to the public but still worth a visit. On the exterior wall a plaque commemorates two brothers, William and David Prosser, who turned their home into this chapel in 1737. It is certainly unusual to see a chapel boasting a chimney! Directly outside the chapel door are rows of gravestones crowding together, colourfully pink with the overlay of centuries of lichen. The graveyard, which is still in use, extends far up the hill and the best view of the chapel is from those upper reaches, with the chapel nestling below.

The Baptist Chapel was also, once, a school. Kilvert recorded how he spent time with one Mrs Jenkins, whose husband had been schoolmaster there. This elderly couple had lived in several places in the Black Mountains and Mrs Jenkins had a treasure trove of tales to tell about strange and wonderful happenings.

So commonly did these things happen that if Mrs Jenkins found herself obliged to walk over the mountains in the dark, she habitually sang hymns, to keep evil at bay.

One night, Mrs Jenkins was walking home from her work, singing a hymn as usual, when she heard a lovelier noise overhead. She fell silent to listen to the sound, which could only be coming from a whole flock of song-birds, but although it was a clear and starry night, she could see no birds overhead. The noise of their singing was travelling in the direction of a certain farm further down the mountain and Mrs Jenkins was left with the certainty that there would soon be a funeral coming from that house. Less than a month later, it came to pass.

Opposite St. Mary's Church is Chapel Farm. It was here that Eric Ravilious (1903 – 1942) stayed for a long period of time, and where he painted his many well-known scenes of Capel y Ffin. Indeed, one of his most famous paintings was of St. Mary's Church itself.

The River Honddu

The River Honddu has its source at the head of the Llanthony Valley and so it is little more than a stream. At Capel y Fffin it is fed by a substantial second stream, Nant Bwch, and many smaller streams wander down the mountainsides on either side to join the Honddu. However, for most of the valley, in summer, the river is shallow and slow-flowing and easy to cross. In several places, fords can be seen even though stone bridges have been built alongside. It is a paradise for children in wellingtons who can spend many happy hours stream-walking.

The grass is very green here and the undergrowth lush; fallen trees lie still until consumed by mosses, fungi and insects, whilst wildlife hides from the walker unless one rests for a while, silently, and waits. Then one might be rewarded by the sight of dragonflies and kingfishers, rabbits and hares, water-voles and dormice and, once darkness begins to fall, foxes, badgers and bats.

The River Honddu is also home to a Ceffyl-dwr; a legendary creature which is a little like the Scottish kelpie. It is a water-horse, the progeny of a fairy horse and a wild fell pony. It is small and grey and inoffensive - but if you do not show it due respect, it will show you even less.

A very old story tells of a man who met the Ceffyl-dwr on the banks of the Honddu near Brecon. He had need to visit Towy, which is near Carmarthen, many miles away, so he told the Ceffyl-dwr and asked for permission to mount him. The Ceffyl-dwr stood quietly while the man climbed on his back - and in a moment, the man found himself in Towy, just where he needed to be.

We have heard, in the stories from Hay, how fairies will quickly end their interactions with humans if they are given any reason to take offence. It will be obvious, then, that a fairy water-horse should be handled very carefully. Unfortunately, the man in our story had not learned this fact.

Three days later, he needed to leave Towy and go home, so he sought out the Ceffyl-dwr. This time, he simply climbed astride the water-horse and told him where he wanted to go, instead of asking. The Ceffyl-dwr did as he was told but this time the journey took much longer and passed through mud and water, thorns and thickets, so that the man arrived back at his home bruised, cut and very dirty.

So if you meet the Ceffyl-dwr one day, remember - ask, don't tell!

Llanthony Tertia Monastery

In April 1870, Kilvert passed this way and noted in his diary that although he had not seen Capel y Ffin for four years, nothing had changed. He was interested to see 'the monks', about whom he had heard so much, and the monastery they were building. He asked directions from a young woman who was doing her washing outside Chapel Farm - he noted her blond hair, blue eyes and clear skin and commented on her 'round, white, lusty' arms covered in soapsuds. Then, following the girl's directions, he went up the lane at the side of the farmhouse and soon found some monks hard at work, trying to turn a field into a garden.

It was a warm day but the monks were fully dressed in their heavy habits, complete with cowls over their heads, looking quite out of place compared to the girl doing her washing or the masons in their comfortable work-clothes. Although the monks must have been aware of being observed, they did not glance in Kilvert's direction and he thought it best not to disturb them. He found a friendlier welcome when he spoke to the masons who were busy laying the foundations of the monastery buildings; they claimed their work would be finished by the end of May (which Kilvert doubted, it now being April) and showed him the original foundation stone which had been laid by Father Ignatius himself a few days previously.

So who, exactly, was Father Ignatius? A complete history of his life can be found in a biography written by Baroness Beatrice de Bertouch, published in 1904. The writing of the book was overseen by Father Ignatius himself and so is not entirely unbiased but, together with other sources, it gives a picture of a very determined man, one who was deeply religious from a young age and who had definite ideas about how that faith should be expressed. He fought to reintroduce the monastic life into the Anglican Church, an ambition which brought him into conflict with authorities all over the country and saw his name in newspaper headlines regularly. However, his preaching style also amassed a huge audience of 'fans' all over the world.

Father Augustine was born Joseph Leycester Lyne in 1837, in London. His wish was to be a monk or a missionary when he grew up. He was encouraged by his mother, but not by his father, who remained resistant to Joseph's ambitions until his death. No doubt his father's opinion was influenced by the many scandals which dogged his son's progress and sparked the above-mentioned scurrilous articles.

Throughout his life, Joseph experienced supernatural happenings, all of which are recorded in de Bertouch's biography.

One evening at his prep school, nine-year-old Joseph was in his dormitory with friends, talking quietly to avoid disturbing a sick boy next door. Suddenly, the door opened and the sick boy came in, asking for the headmaster's wife. Joseph said she was in her room. Then, the boy moved across the room and vanished through the wall! This was witnessed by all eight boys but, the next morning, the headmaster's wife insisted that they could not have seen the boy in question, for he had passed away before their encounter.

As a teenager, Joseph had another strange experience at his school in Spalding. One evening, he went to listen to the choir and settled on the altar steps, his back to the altar. Then he heard a voice saying; "Why do you turn your back upon My altar, poor miserable table though it be, the altar where I Myself am so often present in the sacrament of My Body and Blood?" Certain that he had heard the voice of God, Joseph resolved then to spend his life in religious worship and mission.

When a young man, Joseph was installed as a curate in Plymouth. On one occasion, he spent some time trying to persuade a mother to

baptize her children, but she was resolute. Soon afterwards, one of her daughters was stricken by a sickness which brought her close to death. When Joseph learned about this, he heard again that voice which had spoken to him in the church, telling him to go at once to the child's bedside. This he did and he prayed for the child, who soon recovered in a way which could only be described as miraculous.

Another 'miracle' happened during Joseph's time in Plymouth; he had just left a manuscript with a printer, when a voice told him to go back to the printer's office, at once. There he found a young man writhing on the floor, in the grip of a seizure. His colleagues commented that it was as if he had been possessed by a devil and Joseph, realising why he had been called to return, demanded that the demon should leave the man, 'in the name of Jesus of Nazareth'. At once, the man lay still and calm. He had suffered fits for many years, but never had another attack.

Joseph's first monastic community for men was in Plymouth, in donated premises. Two Brothers moved in and on their first night there, experienced something very strange. One of them awoke to see a faint light outside his room. On investigation, he found a large altar candle, alight and positioned on the stairs. There were only two candles, both of which belonged on the altar. This strange occurrence was interpreted as a sign of divine approval for the community.

In 1862, Joseph went to stay in the East End of London. One night, he and the schoolmaster Joseph Redman were called to see a young woman who was dying of typhoid. Mr Redman took with him a treasured possession; a Relic of the True Cross. On their arrival, they found that the girl had passed away, but Brother Joseph laid the relic on the girl's chest, saying, "In the Name of Jesus Christ, I say unto thee, Arise!" And she did...

It was during his tenure in the East End that Brother Joseph was first taken to Llanthony, during a holiday in the area in 1862. He was captivated by the sight of the ruined Priory and resolved that one day he would rebuild it and establish a monastery there, at some point in the future, when he could raise the funds. For the time being, he accepted an offer from the Rector of Claydon, in Suffolk, where he established a monastic house in a wing of the rectory.

Claydon Rectory was the scene of many angry demonstrations by local people who objected to the presence of the monks; they were disturbed by the sight of monks practicing their faith in a Catholic style, whilst claiming to be Anglican. It soon became necessary to move again, this time to a rambling old mansion, Elm Hill, in Norwich. The monks moved in early in 1863.

Once again, something strange happened very soon after the monks moved into their new home. It was two o'clock in the morning and every single monk was present in chapel to recite Matins - no one was missing - and yet the chapel bell tolled, many times. A little later, a visiting Rector experienced a minor miracle of his own when he witnessed the figure on the chapel crucifix apparently come to life; its eyes opened, its head moved and its loving gaze fell on Brother Ignatius, who was oblivious of the event.

Whilst in Norwich, Brother Joseph effected three more miraculous cures. He gave an epileptic woman some water in which he had dipped a medal of St. Benedict and she never suffered fits again. Secondly, he cured a toothache by giving the sufferer a piece of wool from his own clothing. Lastly, a woman who shouted, 'Curse your bald head!' (referring to his tonsure) was horrified when her small boy lost his hair overnight. She searched for a cure in vain before begging forgiveness from Brother Joseph. Her boy's curls began growing again, at once.

Late one night, Brother Joseph heard a voice telling him to go to the chapel, which he found was ablaze. The voice told him to step into the flames and make the sign of the cross. Wherever he stepped, the flames faded away and he was able to save the chapel from further damage.

During this period the newspapers were full of discourse about Brother Joseph - now Father Ignatius - and his monks. Rumours abounded of unholy things taking place within the monastery. It was time to move on again, this time to Stoke Newington, where another example of miraculous healing occurred. Father Ignatius was summoned to the bedside of a dying woman. She was unable to take food and the doctor was sure she would be dead before morning. Father Ignatius asked the woman if she believed in the Lord. She said she did. And did she believe that Father Ignatius could raise her up? Again, she said she did. Then Father Ignatius said, "In the Name of the Lord Jesus Christ, I say unto thee, arise!" He told the woman's relatives to feed her a steak and bring her to Mass in the morning. She attended Mass, fully recovered. Her shocked doctor, on the other hand, took to his bed for the next six weeks.

In Stoke Newington, Father Ignatius finally set about trying to buy Llanthony Priory but the current owner, Walter Savage Landor, refused to sell. Despite this setback, the Llanthony Valley was still the place where Father Ignatius wished to eventually settle. Eventually he would build his monastery at Capel y Ffin and he would give it the name Llanthony Tertia.

In the meantime, in 1867 the monks moved to a rented property, Laleham Priory, near Staines. Here, a visiting priest asked about a third monk who had been present throughout a service. He would not believe that only two monks had taken part in the ceremony. This ghostly monk is believed to have since appeared numerous times at Llanthony Tertia Abbey, with hands folded and his head covered by his hood.

In the autumn of 1869, financial help from supporters allowed Father Ignatius to buy thirty-three acres of land at Capel y Ffin. Monks came to establish their community a few months later, but it was hardly a triumphant arrival. The site was eleven miles away from the train station and the road passable only by horse and cart. Most of the monks had to walk. Father Ignatius took residence in a shed which doubled as a store-room and the rest of the monks were obliged to sleep in the barn.

Now Father Ignatius was in residence, workmen were found and building began but progress was slow. As autumn came, many monks became ill and were sent away. Two others actually ran away, unable to withstand the privations of this wilderness life. By Advent, the cloister was built but the windows were still unglazed. The monks slept in the barn, which had unglazed windows covered only by blankets to keep the weather out. It was a very uncomfortable winter.

More serious building work began in the spring of 1870. The foundation stone was laid by Father Ignatius on March 17th and the monastery officially named 'Llanthony Monastery of Our Ladye and St. Dunstan, Llanthony Tertia.' By the following Christmas a temporary chapel was in place, complete with a bell, brought from Elm Hill Priory. Yet it was still hard to live in such primitive conditions. Several monks abandoned the place before 1871 drew to a close and it would be several years before the remaining monks could exist in any form of comfort.

It was during this period that Kilvert records a meeting with Father Ignatius, his brother and his parents. He describes the black Benedictine habit Father Ignatius wore, including the knotted rope belt (the knots symbolising his vows), a silver cross around his neck and a rosary of black beads. Kilvert's impression of Father Ignatius was of a gentle, kind man, with a 'saintly' face and beautiful brown eyes. He seemed earnest and single-minded. Father Ignatius' mother was beautiful and clearly held in high regard by the monks, one of whom stared at her adoringly for a long time. Mrs Lyne provided lunch for all those assembled, after which Kilvert was invited to lay a stone in the monastery wall; the building was the long overdue accommodation for the monks. Kilvert commented in his diary how Father Augustine had been too trusting of

the local workmen who, without constant supervision, had worked very slowly indeed.

Another miracle happened in the August of 1873, when a workman was crushed by a falling crate of stones. The many witnesses were sure the man was dead. Father Ignatius brought out a bottle of water from Lourdes, that famous healing spring, and sprinkled it over the 'dead' man, commanding him to arise, in the name of Jesus Christ. And the man scrambled to his feet, apparently whole again.

By far the most famous miracle which occurred at Llanthony Abbey was that which happened on August 30th, 1880. First, an apparition of the Blessed Sacrament manifested outside the Tabernacle doors, so clearly that the Brother who saw it did not question it. That evening, four of the youngest monks saw a shining woman moving across the meadow, her hands held out in blessing. It was the Virgin Mary.

Five days later, two monks saw a bush glowing with light. The two said prayers and sang hymns, hoping that the Virgin Mary would reveal herself again and finally, when they sang the Ave Maria, she did appear, at the top of the meadow by the gate. The light in the bush then took the form of a man dressed only in a loincloth, holding his hands out to the figure of the woman.

It is in honour of this occurrence that a pilgrimage is made every year, through the Llanthony Valley to the Monastery, commemorating the Mother of Jesus' visit to the Abbey Church. There is a life-size statue of the Lady in the spot where she most often appeared.

The 'bush' where the apparition was seen was actually a patch of wild rhubarb. Leaves from this bush were sent to several nuns who were supporters, as souvenirs of the miraculous vision. One of them, Mother Cecilia, suffered constant pain from an abscess on her leg, and one night she prayed earnestly to the Virgin Mary, pressing the leaf from the Holy Bush to her wound. Within days she was walking without the aid of her crutches. Many other cures were reported over the years.

In the spring of 1908 Father Ignatius suffered a severe stroke, followed by another only a few days later. This marked the end of his public appearances, for he remained very unwell for the next seven months. Eventually, with winter approaching and his health still delicate, it was decided that he would benefit from a change of scenery. He spent some time at Sheringham in Norfolk, and then was taken to stay with his sister in Camberley. Whilst there, he suffered a final, fatal stroke and in October 1908, he died. It is sad that Father Ignatius did not pass away in the peace of his own Abbey at Capel y Ffin, but his body was carried back there, to be buried in the Abbey Church.

Eric Gill at The Monastery

After Father Ignatius' death in 1908, the monastery continued to function for some years, becoming dependant on the priory on Caldey Island, according to Father Ignatius' will. It was not a great success, however, and by 1924 the monastery was disbanded and the buildings became the property of the painter and sculptor Eric Gill, who moved there with his family and established a commune for artists and craftsmen. Gill himself was only resident here for four years, leaving in 1928 to set up a lettering workshop in Berkshire, where he designed the typefaces Perpetua and Gill Sans. He died in 1940. The abbey, however, remained in the possession of his family until the 1980s, when his descendants sold the whole property.

Eric Gill was a controversial figure. His unconventional lifestyle is fully described in Fiona MacCarthy's intensive biography, 'Eric Gill' published in 1989. This may have been why he chose to retreat to the isolated location offered by the Monastery, as it gave him the privacy he needed to explore the relationships he wished to pursue. However, despite his immorality, Gill also loved the religious aspect of the Monastery which

allowed him to explore his own sense of religion. He encouraged masses to be held in the chapel for local Catholics. (The church, which had not been well constructed, had begun to crumble.) He resisted modern amenities, adopting a lifestyle appreciated by visiting artists, if not by his family. Conditions were not so different from those the monks had endured; there was no electricity supply and no proper road was constructed through the valley until 1960. Avoiding people was easy and the only visitors were the postman and a doctor who called weekly. There was, however, a ready supply of the raw material necessary for Gill's art; stone in plenty.

The best-known of the artists who joined Gill was his apprentice David Jones, who found his religious faith strengthened during his stay here, as well as his artistic sense. The area inspired him; his paintings of Capel y Ffin and the surrounding landscapes are the best known in his canon.

When Gill and his artist friends moved on, the monastery was transformed into a guesthouse by one of Gill's daughters. It is now owned by a different family, who have converted many of the buildings into holiday apartments. The chapel is open to visitors.

Nant Bwch Waterfall

Continuing along the lane past the Monastery, the route crosses the Nant Bwch stream and then steadily upwards, to the open moorland of the Nant Bwch Valley. The lane, which is passable by car, ends at a farmhouse which is now a co-operative holiday home. Cars can be left on the grass verge and the journey continued on foot.

The path continues past the farmhouse and then for some distance it runs between two stone walls. Finally, after crossing a gated field, you will discover a little treasure in the form of a waterfall. It is not more than ten feet high but it is wide, with a picturesque pool of water at its base. Best seen after rainfall, naturally, but lovely even in dry weather, when the colours of the exposed rocks are strikingly beautiful.

There are many waterfalls in the Black Mountains and the Brecon Beacons; at Tal y Bont the falls are spectacular. But this little waterfall should not be disregarded. It is situated in a delightfully sheltered setting, perfect for an afternoon's rest. The stream, also, is perfect for walking because in many areas its bed is a smooth sheet of stone, very inviting to bare feet.

Bruce Chatwin

One of the best-known fictional works inspired by this area is Bruce Chatwin's novel 'On the Black Hill'. Set in the Llanthony Valley of the 19th and early 20th century, it paints a vivid picture of the strictures and discomforts of farming life in that era. A well-bred governess, suddenly finding herself without any means of support, marries a local farmer. He has a certain charm because of his deep knowledge of the ways of nature, but his new wife soon discovers that he also has a harsh side, a result of the harsh life he leads. The body of the story focuses on their twin sons, who live and grow in this secluded valley and never have the opportunity to move away, sharing their farmhouse and their bedroom until their lives are at an end. Amidst the darkness there are moments of lightness, even comedy, but overall the novel is coloured by the tough lives experienced by those who lived here in those days.

Chatwin first came to the Llanthony Valley with his father, who brought him for a short, impromptu holiday in the car he had just bought. It was an excuse to put the car through its paces, but also an opportunity to introduce Chatwin and his brother to this wonderful countryside. The experience was not wasted on Chatwin, who recalled sleeping in the car and waking next morning to a dew-filled sunrise with sheep all around him, which was a stark contrast to the life he lived in the city. He subsequently visited several times and developed a love for the area which never left him.

When Chatwin came for an extended stay in 1980, he had planned to spend his time writing a short story about two brothers who lived close to his friend, Penelope Betjeman. However, when Penelope introduced him to other families in the area, he found much to inspire him and the story became a novel. Chatwin was entranced by the people he met and also the sense that all who lived here were existing between two worlds; neither truly Welsh nor truly English, the border between the two countries so close at hand that boundaries were blurred.

Kilvert also commented on this when he wrote about a certain cottage which was very much on the border; most of it was in Wales but one corner was in England. Once, a woman in labour here was told to stand in a particular corner when the time came to give birth, so that her child should be born English. Chatwin used this idea in his description of the Vision Farm, where his fictional family lived.

Chatwin was equally impressed by how little life in the valley had been affected by modern invention; things were very much as they had been a century before. He took copious notes of the details of daily life and conversations, so that some of the words uttered by his characters were those he had heard from the neighbouring families, quoted verbatim.

All of this experience, carefully recorded by Chatwin, led to an entrancing novel which easily bears more than one reading. It is absolutely recommended for anyone who has spent time in the Llanthony Valley. For several years, one of the bookshops in Hay-on-Wye had on display a first edition of On The Black Hill, its hefty price of £495 an indication of the value of this work. A film of the book, starring Bob Peck and Gemma Jones, was made in 1987 and features a wonderful aerial tour of the valley.

The Vision Farm in the novel was based on an actual farm of that name, situated near the monastery at Capel y Ffin. It was, of course, named after the famous vision of the Virgin Mary.

Llanthony Priory

In April 1870, after visiting the Monastery at Capel y Ffin, Kilvert walked on to Llanthony Priory. He might have written more about the beautiful building, the picturesque setting, the tranquil atmosphere but he was distracted by two loud-voiced tourists, one of whom was lecturing the other and pointing out details with a stick. Any of us would find such people annoying but Kilvert was appalled; in his diary, he described them venomously as 'vulgar, ill-bred, offensive and loathsome'!

The story of Llanthony Priory starts with St. David's Church, which stands next to the ruins of the priory. It is reputed to have been built on the site of a monastic cell inhabited by Wales' patron saint, St. David. It is said that David came here in the 6th century. At this time, the Romans had left these shores and the invading Saxons were driving the Celts deeper into the west of the country, so the above supposition may well be true. The name Llanthony is a derivation of the original ancient place-name Llan-ddewi-nant-honddu, which translates as 'the clan of Saint David on the river Honddu'.

As the centuries rolled by the original cell fell into disuse. Then came the Norman invasion. William DeLacey, a relative of the Lord of Ewyas, came across this place on a hunting expedition. Charmed by the peaceful atmosphere of the spot, as well as the little monastic cell, which was almost in ruins and covered in ivy and moss, he decided to renovate the cell as a chapel, live there and adopt a life of prayer and contemplation.

He was joined in 1103 by Ernisius, chaplain to Queen Maud, who was likewise charmed by the holy atmosphere he found here. The two men pooled their resources and built a small church, which was dedicated in 1108. Very soon they were joined by others and the Archbishop of Canterbury agreed to the establishment of a Priory of Augustinian monks, known as the Black Canons because of their adopted black clothing. The construction of the original Priory buildings was complete by 1120.

The original Priory was active for only a few years, as the country remained in the throes of political unrest with great trouble between the Normans and the Welsh. For many years the Priory stood empty as the community was forced to retreat to a safer location on English soil. Then, around 1180, a new round of construction began, notably on the huge church dedicated to St. Mary, John the Baptist and Saint Florence, with other necessary monastic buildings being erected at the same time.

It was during this period that the present St. David's Church was built, on the site of the original church built by William DeLacey and Ernisius.

It is interesting to note that, just as stone circles were designed to align with celestial bodies so that midwinter or midsummer sunrises illuminated precise spots, so early Christian churches were aligned in the same way. St. David's Church is built so that the altar points directly to the spot where the sun rises on St. David's Day, March 5th. In the same way, the Priory Church, dedicated to St. John, is aligned to the sunrise on St. John's Day, June 24th.

The Priory was a successful establishment and received many gifts, from small contributions of food or money to larger donations of land, which increased the Priory's value and its influence. The Priory was also awarded rights to take fish from Llangorse Lake and install them in the Priory fishponds; they were caught and carried in wet rushes, to keep them alive.

The Priory was active for four centuries and then, in the 15th century, revolution came. The Welsh Rebellion was led by Owain Glyndwr, intent on reclaiming Welsh land from the English.

Most of the monks were forced to retreat, some to Hereford and others to their sister abbey, Llanthony Secunda, in Gloucester. By the time Henry VIII was set upon his path of dissolving the monasteries throughout his kingdom, there were only four Black Canons still in residence at Llanthony. They were pensioned off and the site was sold for £160. The Priory would never be active as a religious house again. Then began the centuries of crumbling and ruin which led to the picturesque remains visible today.

In 1809, the whole Priory estate, including Cwmyoy and Llanthony, was bought by Walter Savage Landor, the Romantic poet. He lived in one of the Priory's towers at first, before building a mansion whose remains are just behind Wiral Wood, above the Priory. Landor named the place Siarpal, after the pre-existing farm which had stood there. The name came from a feature in the hill above the farm, Cwm Siarpal, the first part of the name, 'siarp' literally meaning 'sharp'.

Landor, then aged thirty-two, adopted the stance of a country squire and set about 'improving' the landscape around Siarpal and the priory with hundreds of cedar, beech and larch trees. He constructed useful new roads through the valley and across the hillsides. He also attempted to modernise local agricultural methods and imported new breeds of sheep, although these ideas were not welcomed.

However, Landor's enthusiasm - and his funds - lasted for only five years, at which point he left the area, disgusted with the resistance of the local people to the changes he felt were essential to their lives and economy. It is safe to say that his presence in the valley had never been entirely welcome. The Landor family continued to own the lands but were very much absentee landlords. Landor's mansion fell into ruins but in recent years it has been renovated, so Walter Savage Landor's influence will not be entirely forgotten. Landor's time at Siarpal was later fictionalised in Iain Sinclair's novel, *Landor's Tower*.

The ruins of Llanthony Priory are said to be haunted by ghostly monks - one has been seen walking down the hill to the stream, to wash himself in the Monk's Pool.

Above the priory, the mountain is the setting for a ghost story about a man who was walking from Llanthony to Longtown when a thick fog descended, causing him to lose his way. Then he saw another man, a ghostly form in cloak and hat, who beckoned. Following him, the man was soon back on the familiar path but his helper had vanished. His friends in Llanthony, on hearing his description of the man, told him he was known to them - but that he had died two years before.

Wiral Wood, just above the priory, is also said to be haunted. The ghost is a witch, who sometimes appears as herself, wearing her black shawl, or sometimes as a crow. Once, a shepherd driving his flock down the mountain shouted at an old woman who was standing in his way and frightening his sheep. Then, suddenly, she was no longer there. From that point on, however, the shepherd's flock was followed by a large crow who flew angrily at the sheep, repeatedly. Only when the flock crossed a stream did the crow stop following and this was proof that the crow was actually an evil spirit, because evil spirits cannot cross water. So, the crow must have been the old woman in another form and the old woman herself, a witch!

The shepherd was not the only person to meet with the Wiral Wood witch. A group of children playing in the woods were frightened by her one day and a rector of Llanthony once saw her, by moonlight, surrounded by the misty forms of the dead with whom she was conversing. His first response, as a clergyman, was to cross himself but he feared that this Christian blessing was not enough to avert the evil influence he had witnessed. To be sure, when he reached his home he reverted to the older, superstitious customs by placing a lit candle in his window and tying a red ribbon on his baby's cradle to keep her safe.

Another local legend tells of a secret passage somewhere amongst the buildings at Llanthony. The passage leads all the way under the mountain to Longtown Castle, where the explorer will find a hoard of treasure. It was said that a dog was once sent down this passage and was not seen again until several days later, when he emerged at the other end of the tunnel, starving and weak.

Somewhere in the vicinity of the Priory there is rumoured to be a well, although I confess I have never found it. It was known as Our Lady's Workhouse and its water was said to have medicinal properties. Many sick people who bathed there were healed.

The evocative ruins of Llanthony Priory are open to the public, from 10 am to 4 pm daily, all year round. Entry is free and there is an ample car park. There is a hotel on the site and a curious café in the vaulted cellar.

For the best view of the Priory in its entirety, walk around the hotel and along the path which leads into the field beyond.

Cwmyoy

Continuing along the road after Llanthony, it is worth taking a detour to visit Cwmyoy. This tiny settlement can be seen from the road, perched on the mountainside with St. Martin's Church as its focus. The name, Cwmyoy, means 'vale of the yoke' and the mountain here is indeed the shape of a yoke, the curve an indicator of how the mountainside has slowly slipped and changed its form. This gentle subsidence has affected St. Martin's Church to that it is now charmingly crooked and supported by several sturdy stone buttresses.

At first sight the road leading to Cwmyoy appears to lead solely to a large private house but, in fact, the lane passes between two separate buildings and onwards. A stone bridge crosses the River Honddu and then the lane leads upwards, first through a tunnel of trees and then between high green hedges. Be warned that the last stretch of road, leading up to the church, is very steep but behind the church itself there is a small space where cars can be parked.

View the church from the gate in the wall and it is clear just how crooked the church has become. Alternatively, walk on past the gate and down the hill to the other entrance, where you will approach the church along a path of paving stones, several of which are engraved with a single word... reading one's way along the path, it becomes clear that it is actually a unique memorial.

Inside the church porch is a wonderful plaque, centuries old and made up of symbols which are more than simply decorative. Harvest and fertility are indicated by sheaves of grain, but the anchors indicate 'hope, the anchor of the soul'; an ancient symbol for Christ as the anchor of faith. The hearts, crosses and anchors also refer to the triad of love. The plaque bears a large central stylised cross, which is slightly crooked, just like the church it adorns.

The church's roof has been dated to be seven centuries old, but the body of the church is much older - the font is certainly Norman.

A charming tradition says that the hillside's slow subsidence, leading to the church's crookedness, was caused by an earthquake which happened at the very time Christ was being crucified.

This crookedness leads to an unnerving view down the aisle; the chancel leans to the right and the bell-tower to the left, so badly that only two of the bells can actually be rung.

Taking pride of place inside the church is a medieval cross, thought to have been one of many roadside crosses along the Pilgrim's Way leading to the town of St. David's. A spotlight gives a better view of the carving on the cross, which shows a detailed figure of Christ on the cross, wearing a crown of thorns.

Also of note are the several memorial plaques which decorate the walls and surround the windows. Those around the window on the left of the photo below describe a sad and touching history of one particular family. Notice also the lintel above this window, for some colourful medieval paintwork can still be seen.

Leave Cwmyoy by travelling along the road leading left - the lane eventually rejoins the main road through the valley.

Crickhowell and Llangattock

Crickhowell is a pretty riverside town with a wealth of shops, cafes and pubs. The Bear Hotel, in the centre, is popular with walkers. Crickhowell's older name is Crug Hywel, after the mountain of the same name which overlooks the town. Crug Hywel is known in English as Table Mountain and its flat top can be seen in the background of the photo above. This flat area is the site of an Iron Age Celtic hillfort and is easily accessible by footpaths from the town.

Crickhowell boasts a 14th century church, St. Edmund's, the ruins of a castle and a 16th century bridge with twelve arches, crossing the River Usk. On Tower Street can be seen the remains of two drum towers, long assumed to have been the gateway to the town, which was surrounded by walls in the 13th century.

St. Edmund's Church was established in 1303 by the owner of Crickhowell Castle, the widowed Lady Sybil Pauncefote. Lady Pauncefote was English, which may explain why this is the only church in Wales dedicated to this English saint, who was the patron saint of England at the time. Look closely at Lady Pauncefote's effigy within the church and you will notice that it has no hands. The legendary explanation for this is that she gave her hands as ransom for her husband's life when he was imprisoned during the Crusades.

On the other side of the river from Crickhowell lies the village of Llangattock, named for St. Catwg. Llangattock is a largely residential village, made up of 18th and 19th century houses with some older examples. In the middle of the village is a tree-covered mound, known as Garn Goca, which is actually a Bronze Age barrow.

St. Catwg's Church is a fine 14th century building, with later additions; Tudor and Elizabethan features abound. This is another church where the churchyard is almost circular, indicating that the site may have been used for religious ritual since ancient, pre-Christian, times. A church has stood in this place since at least the 6th century. There are some very interesting memorials inside the church including one which remembers a midwife, Anne Lewis, who brought 713 children into the world! The old village stocks and whipping post are displayed in the north aisle.

There are several stories of ghosts and superstition attached to Llangattock. A bridge which carries the canal over a brook is locally known as The Devil's Arch. A lane which passed Tyle Barn was long thought to be haunted (there may have been a murder there) and local people would not use the lane at night. Particularly interesting are the old tales of a spectral black dog frightening horses; it was reported on several of the local roads. This dog was thought to be the mythical Cwn Annwn, which was said to be the Devil in animal form.

Cwn Annwn are variously described as ugly black dogs with red patches in their coat, or little white dogs with glittering eyes. Other stories say they have red coats with black spots. They travel in packs, sometimes in the company of their master, Arawn, the King of the Underworld, who is swarthy and huge, carrying a horn around his neck and a hunting-pole across his back. Arawn rides a grey horse and sometimes he is accompanied by Mallt y Nos, Matilda of the Night, who drives the hounds onward. Matilda is said to be the ghost of a Norman woman who, hearing that there was no hunting in heaven, decided she would rather not go. Condemned to a half-life, then, she wails in misery as she hunts through the night, forever.

The hounds are usually heard before they are seen, but those who follow the baying and howling will soon die, as will those who are followed by the hounds, because they pursue their quarry in silence.

Elsewhere in the Llangattock area, there was once a fairy ring on a piece of land known as the 'Black Turf'. Local people kept away, because they knew that those foolish enough to enter a fairy ring would lose all sense of time and may even be lost forever. There was another fairy ring in a field known as the Devil's Ridge, above Llangattock Park, from which the Devil himself was said to emerge. Also, the house in Llangattock Park was haunted by ghostly footsteps. A local doctor was called there one Midsummer's Eve and when midnight arrived, he clearly heard footsteps progressing upwards through the house.

In the old days, Llangattock people talked about the 'corpse candle'; a strange light which would be seen travelling towards the churchyard, foretelling a death. In 1872, a phantom funeral was seen moving along a lane by a labourer returning from his daily work. The strangest thing was that the procession was moving along in mid-air. A few days later, a funeral procession did indeed travel down that lane, which was so full of snow that the mourners were walking above the hedges...

On Llangattock Mountain, above the village, there is a pool called Pwll Gwy-rhoc, the Witches' Pool. It is an eerie place, as the name suggests. It is said that the water sometimes appears to be the colour of blood, because the five great Welsh tribes once fought a terrible battle here. So churned was the ground that it became very boggy and eventually sank to become a lake. In truth, it is now believed that there really was once a battle here, between the men of Mercia and Morgannwg, which resulted in a massive defeat for the Mercians.

A strange story is told about one Richard the Tailor, who was once the landlord of a Llangattock inn and had long been suspected of practicing occult arts. The story tells of a hunting party who were pursuing a hare, which escaped through an open window into Richard the Tailor's inn. Weary from their chase, the hunters decided to rest a while at the Inn, but did so grudgingly as several of them believed that the hare had been Richard the Tailor himself, bent on luring them and their money to his establishment, when it was too late to do anything other than stay for the night.

During the evening, one of the party, Walter Jones, excused himself to go outside, just for a few minutes, but he did not return until the next morning.

He was exhausted and terrified, his clothes torn and in disarray. The story he told was remarkable: the minute he left the Inn, he said, he was grabbed by invisible hands which dragged him along the lanes all night, depositing him twenty miles away at a place near Newport, where he was ordered to help a man lift bags of coal onto his horse's back. Then suddenly it was morning and he was outside the Inn once again! The story goes on to explain that Walter Jones had always been dissolute in his habits, but that after his experience he was a changed man.

The start of that story, about a human turning into a hare, meaning that she is a witch, is a motif in folk tales all over England but this is the first time I have heard it told in Wales. In my home county of Lancashire, the story features an old woman called Marjorie Hilton, who wanted a certain cottage so much that she challenged the Landlord to a race; she would race to the cottage against his hounds, and if she won, he would let her live there. The Landlord agreed not to release his fastest hound but, of course, did not keep to his agreement. Marjorie turned herself into a hare and soon lost all the hounds, apart from the fastest one, who managed to nip one of the hare's back feet, just before it leapt through the cottage window. Marjorie won her bet and moved into her cottage but it was noticed that she walked with a limp for many days afterwards.

Compare this story featuring a farmer who lived at the foot of the Black Mountain. He bred greyhounds for the gentry and would allow local boys to race them for fun and exercise. One day, the hounds found a hare under a bush and were about to seize it when one of the local boys shouted, 'Run, Grannie, run, the hounds be after thee!' The hare ran to a cottage and went through the keyhole, but not before one of the hounds bit her on the leg. When the boys went to retrieve their hounds, they found an old woman sitting by the fire and tending to her leg, which was bleeding.

With so many tales of otherworldly happenings in Llangattock, it is hardly surprising to find that certain old-time residents also reported having seen the most famous ghost in the Black Mountains area; the Old Woman of the Mountain.

One report came from a well-respected local man, one Robert Williams, who was walking over the Black Mountain one night when he lost his way and, seeing a woman a little distance away, called to her for assistance and directions. When she did not respond, Williams thought she might be deaf and began to run in an attempt to catch up to her. No matter how fast he ran, he found he could not reach her.

Finally, he found himself stranded in a marsh, with the Old Woman's cackling laughter ringing in his ears. It was that sound which made him realise that she might be a ghost. He drew out his knife, knowing that ghosts and fairies are afraid of knives and, sure enough, the Old Woman vanished at the very sight of it.

Finally, we cannot leave Llangattock without a mention of the Piccy Stone, also known as the Peaky Stone. Both versions of this name may well originate from the Welsh word 'pwca' which means ghost or fairy.

This shaft of limestone, which stands on Llangattock Mountain, is also sometimes referred to as 'The Lonely Shepherd.' The tale behind this name explains that the shepherd was turned to stone as punishment for mistreating his wife, who eventually drowned herself in the River Usk. It is said that at midnight every Midsummer's Eve the stone goes down to the river to look for the drowned wife. This tale led to a charming tradition where the women of Llangattock would walk up to the Lonely Shepherd on Midsummer's Eve, to make it ready for its journey down to the river by whitewashing it and dressing it in men's clothing.

Llangynidr

A little distance from Llangattock and Crickhowell is Llangynidr, which is included here simply for the pleasure of relating the following tale. The Rev. Elwyn Thomas was a Wesleyan minister at Llangynidr and his ghost story first appeared in print in 1915, in a very respected journal. His experience had happened one evening in 1903, after an evening service. He had met up with some friends who were visiting from Crickhowell and when they set off for home, he walked with them for a while.

After parting from his friends, Rev. Thomas walked alone for a while and then he saw an old man who looked like a beggar. He wondered where the man had come from and as he looked more closely he was shocked at the sight of the old man's face, which looked for all the world like that of a corpse; colourless, with bloodless lips and sunken cheeks. The eyes were set back in the man's skull and they stared at the Reverend in a particularly piercing and unsettling way. The Reverend had plenty of time time to note the man's appearance and strange dress, which included two strips of yellow calico, one of which was wrapped around the man's face from his chin to the top of his head. The other was wound around the man's forehead and fastened at the back.

Horrified, the Reverend ran away, then turned to find the ghastly man still there, right behind him! He lifted his umbrella to strike the man but now saw only a cloudy column - which his umbrella passed straight through. He ran again and stopped several yards away, only to see the man standing by the churchyard's yew tree, where he disappeared.

The Reverend was so shocked by his experience that he could not speak of it for several days and could only lay in his bed, too distressed to move. When he did eventually recover, he told his friends the story, describing the man's dress, his face, his yellow calico bands... only to be told that this was a description of an old eccentric, long dead, who had lived in a house very near the spot where the ghost had disappeared.

The Reverend Thomas was so affected by his experience that he reported it to the Society of Psychical Research, in London, who took his story seriously. So seriously, in fact, that the case was included in Hereward Carrington's collection 'True Ghost Stories', which was published in 1915.

Patrishow

Another worthwhile detour off the main valley road, in the same direction as Crickhowell, is the tiny settlement of Patrishow. The church of St. Issui is the stopping-place. The spot is as remote as it could be, the lanes leading there as narrow and steep as anywhere yet experienced, the view over the Grwne Fawr Valley impressive. But the church is the treasure we are seeking.

When first visiting, one immediately wonders why a church would be built in this inaccessible place? The reason lies in the legend of St. Issui, the Celtic saint after whom the church is named. Issui lived in the 6th century and was a simple religious hermit whose dwelling place was below the church, close to St. Mary's Stream.

There is space to park cars where the road bends, close to the stream; crossing the lane there will bring you to the holy well which marks the place where Issui spent his time. The well is actually a spring feeding a small pool and long ago it was enclosed in a little stone structure which still survives. Visitors leave offerings on a slab of stone by the spring; pebbles, leaves, small treasures they have brought in memory of loved ones. A nearby tree bears remnants of strips of cloth, following an old tradition where a scrap of clothing taken from a sick person's body and hung on the tree would, by a kind of sympathetic magic, effect healing. More noticeable are the hundreds of coins which have been forced into the tree, some so old that the tree has grown around them. These are offerings to the spirit of the well, for the simple reward of safe travel.

St. Issui, after whom the well is named, was a mild man, respected for his willingness to share what little. One day, he gave food to a traveller but instead of thanking him, the traveller attacked and killed the peaceful hermit, leaving his broken body in the well.

When the hermit's body was discovered, arrangements were made for him to be buried at the top of the hill and people began to come to visit his grave and also the well, whose water soon became attributed with the ability to heal many illnesses. In the 11th century, a certain man made the pilgrimage to the well, having exhausted all other remedies. He was suffering from leprosy and, incredibly, the water cured him. So grateful was this man that he donated 'a hat-full of gold', so that a church might be built nearby.

And so the Church of St. Issui was built, directly over his grave, which is under the altar in the tiny cell-like chapel. The doorway is 14th century, the wooden door a remarkable survival. The tiny, crooked lancet window is a century older, its angle caused by subsidence. An open grille above the tomb allows those in the chapel to hear mass being said.

Most of the architecture here dates from the 13th and 14th centuries, but older churches existed. The font in the main church is definitely from the 11th century, as the inscription around its lip states 'Menhir made me in the time of Genillin'. Genillin (or Cynhillin) is mentioned in records of 1056 and was the son of the Lord of the surrounding area. This font is all that remains of the original church which was dedicated by Herewald before the Norman invasion.

The font is not the only treasure here. The 16th century wall paintings are a wonder. They include a marvellous doom figure on the rear wall; a life-size figure of a skeleton, holding a scythe, an hour-glass and a spade. It is said to have been painted in ox blood so that despite many coats of whitewash, it always shows through the paint, in time. Other paintings feature the Royal Coat of Arms of Charles II and Protestant texts from the Bible and Prayer Book, including the Creed and Decalogue. Charmingly, these texts also show errors on the part of the painter - a word missed from the original has been added later, above the line...

The carved wooden rood screen is dated to around 1500 AD and boasts beautiful tracery. The workmanship is so fine that it has been suggested it could only have been the work of the Flemish, who were skilled in the art, but really there is no reason to think Welsh craftsmen were not responsible. A band of ornamental carving running along the top features a wyvern (a dragon with only two legs) at either end. Also featured are representations of St Mary the Virgin, and St John the Apostle.

Outside the church, the churchyard boasts a 14th century preaching cross, a miraculous survival from Henry VIII's decree that all such crosses should be destroyed. Most of the gravestones date from the 18th and 19th centuries but are interesting for those who enjoy studying such inscriptions. Finally, for those wondering what purpose could have been served by the little stone lean-to next to the church, it is said to have been used to shelter the horses used by priests who served this church but lived some distances away.

Llanvihangel Crucorney

At we reach the end of the Llanthony Valley we come to the little settlement of Llanvihangel Crucorney. This settlement is overlooked by the Sugarloaf Mountain and the Skirrid, both of which feature in a folktale about Jack o' Kent, a hero who often outsmarted the Devil. He once had an argument with the Devil, claiming that the Sugarloaf was higher than the Malvern Hills. When the Devil found Jack o' Kent was right, he gathered an enormous amount of soil and rocks in his apron, intending to use them to make the Malvern Hills higher, but his apron strings snapped mid-flight and his load was dropped on the Skirrid. As evidence, the Skirrid still has a large mound on one side.

Another story says that the mound was caused when the Devil offered bribes and promises to St. Michael, if he would follow the Devil's own evil path. Naturally, St. Michael could not be persuaded. Finally, the Devil lost his temper and stamped his foot, causing many loose rocks to fall down the hillside and form the mound we see today.

The western side of the Skirrid has a huge cleft, caused by Jack o' Kent's foot as he leapt onto the mountain from the Sugarloaf. Once on the Skirrid, he began to throw stones from the top of the mountain, to see how far he could throw them. He managed to throw three stones as far as Trelleck and they are still there, standing together in a field. He threw another but not quite so far and that, too, is still there to this day, known by the name the Pecked Stone (pecked meaning 'thrown').

The Skirrid takes its name from the Welsh, Ysgyryd, which means 'divided' and refers to the afore-mentioned cleft. It is also known as the Holy Mountain, because a legend says that the earthquake and the rift happened at the very time when Christ was being crucified – the same legend used to explain the crooked state of the church at Cwmyoy.

The soil on the hill is extremely fertile and so, in the old days, it was regarded as holy in itself. Sacks of it would be brought from the hill to scatter on fields to ensure good crops and it was also sprinkled on coffins at Catholic funerals. Many parish churches in the county are built on foundations which include soil taken from the mountain. It is also said that no worms or snails exist on the mountain, for the very reason that it is holy and so they cannot live there.

There was once a church on the summit of the Skirrid, named after St. Michael. Nothing now remains of the old church apart from two boulders which mark the old entrance but it was frequently used in times past, until at least the beginning of the 18th century. Pilgrimages would be made to the summit of the hill to St. Michael's Church on September 28th, Michaelmas Eve.

Also on the summit are the remains of an Iron Age hillfort and a large stone known as the Devil's Table.

Returning to Jack o' Kent, this is one folkloric character who actually did exist. Father John of Kentchurch was born in the 15th century and was a Franciscan, an academic and also a bard. Such learned people were often regarded as wizards or having dealings with the Devil. However, the stories told about him and the Skirrid sound older, so it's quite likely that they were first told about some older character.

There are many other stories about Jack o' Kent and his dealings with the Devil. According to the stories, the pair first became linked when Jack was still just a child and the two of them made a pact. The Devil gave Jack the power to achieve anything he set his mind to and, in return, he promised that the Devil should take his soul when he died.

One day, when Jack was still a young boy, he had been told to keep the crows off the crops, but he badly wanted to go to the nearby fair. So he used his powers to call all the crows from the fields into a barn, where he shut them in and went off to the fair. The barn was old and had no roof but, even so, when Jack returned all the crows were still there, just where he had told them to stay.

Another time, Jack bet the Devil that if they shared the harvest from a certain field, Jack would get a bigger share. He knew the field was full of turnips, but the Devil did not, and all that could be seen were the tops of the plants. Asked if he wanted the tops or the bottoms, the Devil naturally said the tops - and lost the bet. The following year, the Devil took Jack's bet again but said he would take the bottoms. Jack planted wheat in the field, so the Devil lost again!

When Jack came to the end of his life, the Devil was determined to take his soul in payment for the powers he had given Jack and, also, as retribution for all the tricks Jack had played on him over the years. He said Jack could not escape even by being buried inside a church; inside or outside, he would take Jack's soul. But Jack beat him again, by being buried half inside and half outside, under the wall of Grosmont Church.

One last story from the Skirrid mountain features a 'cunning man' who once lived there. He was well-known for many miles around and always willing to help anyone who called on him. He insisted that payment for his services be left on a certain large stone, not given to him directly, and it was said that coins would disappear from that stone without the cunning man being anywhere close. Many people were willing to testify that this was a fact!

In the village of LLanvihangel Crucorney itself is the beautiful building known as Llanvihangel Court. This Tudor manor house is privately owned but is open for guided tours for a few days each summer. It still boasts 15th century panelling, an oak staircase and a 17th century plaster ceiling. The house is magnificently decorated. It is also famous for the many ancient Spanish chestnut trees in the grounds, which are reputed to have been brought here from Spain at the time the house was built.

It is said that King Charles I visited here during the Civil War and the bed in which he slept is lovingly preserved, in the 'King's Room'. There are also two wonderful staircases, one of oak in the oldest part of the building and another, of yew, in a wing which was added in the 17th century. On the latter staircase, it is said that three of the stairs bear stains which cannot be removed, the result of a fight to the death on the landing above.

In the White Room, visitors to the house have reported seeing a small, ghostly man with green skin and eyes. A most peculiar description!

Another ghost, a 'white lady', has long been said to walk out of the house and into a wooded area which can be seen from the terrace. The Welsh author F.J. Hando once asked a guide if he had ever seen the white lady; the guide replied that he had not, but that his father had experienced something very strange. Late one night, his father and the chauffeur had been sitting in one of the downstairs rooms, talking. Suddenly they saw the door open and then close and then they heard the external door do the same thing. It was one o'clock in the morning but this was in summertime and the 'real' time was midnight, exactly when the white lady was said to walk. The guide's father had also heard, on another occasion, a woman's scream.

Not far away is the Skirrid Mountain Inn, which claims to be the oldest pub in Wales. Records dating from 1100 AD mention the Inn, although the present building is probably Elizabethan. There is a great deal of interesting history connected to the Inn. The mounting block outside the main door is said to have been used by Owain Glyndwr when he was summoning support for the Welsh Revolt against Henry IV. Also, for many years the Skirrid was used as a courtroom where harsh justice was meted out. Ropemarks can still be seen on a joist above the stairwell.

Over 180 people were sentenced to death here and many of their ghosts are said to haunt the place. Visitors sometimes report feeling a rope around their neck when they are walking up the stairs. A room on the first floor is said to be haunted by a convict who some say was the very first criminal to be hanged at the Skirrid, a sheep rustler called John Crowther. Other ghosts have been named as Father Henry Vaughn, who lived locally, and Fanny Price, a servant who died of consumption in the 18th century, in what is now Room 3. The Inn has hosted many ghost-hunts over the years and the list of experiences grows. Whilst some of these experiences may owe much to imagination, it cannot be denied that many people have had scary experiences here.

Some have heard soldiers and horses in the Inn's courtyard, while others report hearing the rustling sound of a woman's silk dress, accompanied by a cold draught. Some smell perfume. Some glimpse a ghostly woman. Those who feel a noose around their necks sometimes have marks left on their skin; others who use the staircase suffer nausea and dizziness. Footsteps and knocking sounds have been heard and some people have reported seeing faces looking in at the windows. Perhaps the most worrying experience was that of a woman guest who ran downstairs, still wet from her bath, shouting, 'She tried to drown me!'

One of the most famous residents of Llanfihangel Crucorney was the novelist and noted academic Raymond Williams, who was born here in 1921. His political leanings were Marxist in tone and he was most definitely a Welsh Nationalist. In addition, today's academic field of 'cultural studies' was largely founded on his work and opinions. Towards the end of his life, he began work on a series of novels set in the area where he had grown up, entitled People of the Black Mountains. He died in 1988 without completing the work but the first two novels were published after his death by his wife.

The novels imagine the history of the peoples of the Black Mountains from Paleolithic times up to the Middle Ages. They are all the more fascinating because they focus on ordinary people and the events depicted are solidly based on historical facts and archaeological evidence. Arguably the most oft-quoted passage describes how one can map the valleys of the Black Mountains using the back of one's right hand; fingers denote the mountain ranges and the gaps between them the valleys and their streams. It is the clearest way to imagine the Black Mountain area. Incidentally, the Llanthony Valley lies between your first and second fingers.

Abergavenny

Just a short distance from Llanvihangel Crucorney is the much larger town of Abergavenny. In this lovely market town, there is much to see. The entries below provide just a glimpse of what the place has to offer; Abergavenny does not really belong in a book about the Llanthony Valley, but it is hard to leave it out entirely.

Abergavenny's castle was established in 1087 and was always a fortress rather than a noble's family home. It has seen much violence through the centuries; in 1175 it was the scene of a dreadful massacre of Welsh nobles and during the 15th century it was attacked during the Welsh Rebellion led by Owain Glyndwr. What remains has been a listed building since 1952 and is now set in formal gardens and walks, open to the public. There is also an entertaining museum, housed in the 19th century gatehouse which was built on top of the motte.

The castle was built on the site of an older fortress which, according to legend, was built by the giant Gigas Orgo. This is worth noting because

Gigas Orgo was the only giant mentioned in Monmouthshire's folklore.

There is said to be a tunnel beneath Abergavenny Castle which stretches as far as that which runs between Llanthony and Longtown. One man, a long time ago, claimed to have found the tunnel and had ventured along it for a while but was too nervous to go any further. This particular tunnel, sadly, was actually a wine cellar, with very definite boundaries.

Abergavenny's magnificent Priory Church, St. Mary's, was founded in 1087. It houses some remarkable treasures including a 15th century sculpture of Jesse, who was father to King David and thus an ancestor of Jesus. Once, the wooden figure was the base for an enormous sculpture showing all of Jesse's descendants on the branches of a tree standing between twenty and thirty feet tall, with Christ at the top. The surviving single figure, carved from a single piece of oak, is now housed below a glorious 'Jesse Window', which depicts the whole of Christ's lineage.

The plinth supporting the figure of Jesse was designed by German cabinetmaker Joachim Tantau and the Jesse Window was designed by Helen Whittaker. A very interesting booklet available at the church describes both artists' work in detail. The Window was installed in 2016, in memory of a much loved Dean, Jeremy Winston. HRH The Prince of Wales attended the ceremony.

Be prepared to lose an hour as you explore the Priory Church because it is home to many beautiful monuments and tombs, one of which boasts four green men. They are tricky to spot on this highly decorated 16th century monument, but once the first is identified, the others become obvious to the eye. The choir stalls date from the 14th century and host several charming carvings of dragons and other mythical creatures.

Leaving the Priory Church behind, just outside Abergavenny there was once a well, beside the New Monmouth Road, whose water was good for sore eyes. Pins were left herel as offerings to the spirits of the water.

As for ghosts... whilst no ghosts are reported at the Priory or the Castle, there are many in Abergavenny. The best known is at the King's Arms, a pub dating from 1400, where a ghostly old lady in black has often been seen walking down the staircase and through the lounge.

There is also another ghost haunting the King's Arms, that of a scullery maid who served here in the 16th century. At that time there were underground tunnels connecting Abergavenny Castle to the Priory Church and also to the King's Arms. One night, a renegade monk came down this tunnel from the Priory and seriously assaulted the young scullery maid. Now, her ghost wanders the corridors and has often been reported appearing in one of the bedrooms known as the Red Room. One resident woke to find the young woman leaning over her and found herself saying out loud, 'You stay away from my husband!'

Myths and Folklore

There is a wealth of folklore which is common to this area, rather than being attached to any particular place. For much of what follows, we must thank our old friend Francis Kilvert, who so carefully recorded his conversations and recorded these lovely tales in his diaries.

More than once, Francis Kilvert visited 'old Hannah', listening to the stories she had heard as a small girl, told by her grandparents who had heard the stories themselves as children, at the start of the 18th century. They spoke of Hob who would lead folk astray with his lantern, and how children would wear their hats backwards when passing a fairy ring as a protection against the fairies who might tempt them into their ring and dance them to death. One story told of a man who was on his way home from Hay Fair and, being the worse for drink, was tempted by the fairy music and stepped inside the ring to dance. He danced and danced for what must have been years, for when he eventually stopped and left the ring and went to his home, his family had all gone...

Much folklore deals with the healing qualities of plants and the superstitions surrounding their collection and preparation. Those who worked with medicinal plants understood the best conditions for their collection and preparation but these conditions seemed mysterious, even magical, to the uninformed. Thus they passed into folklore and became superstitions. Sometimes these superstitions had sensible reasoning behind them, sometimes not. For example, it is said that blackberries should never be collected after October 31st because after that, the Devil spits on them!

In the old days, many people believed in the power of magical charms which were trusted to bring relief from common ailments. One such charm, to relieve toothache, was written on a paper to be carried by the afflicted and read:

"As Peter stood at the gate of Jerusalem, Jesus saith unto him, 'What aileth thee?' He said, 'My teeth do ache.' Jesus said, 'Whosoever carrieth these lines about them, or beareth them in memory, shall never have the toothache any more, in the name of the Father, and of the Son, and of the Holy Ghost, Amen! and Amen! So be it according to thy faith."

Those who were able to heal were often regarded as witches but their powers were simply a deep knowledge of the healing qualities of plants and herbs. However, a few people were thought to have more unusual healing abilities, mainly the ability to stem the flow of blood from cuts. Such healers were always in demand as their reputations spread far and wide.

The fear of death was ever-present and folklore records several beliefs around this topic. There are several tales of 'phantom funerals'; one example tells of a lady who was walking into Hay and had to pause to allow a funeral to pass by. She watched its slow progression and was later able to describe in detail the cloaks and hatbands worn by the followers. When she reached Hay she asked who had died but no-one knew of any death, or funeral, and no-one had seen the procession enter the town. The lady was left with the disturbing certainty that she had seen a phantom funeral, which foretold a death in her own family.

Another omen of an impending death and funeral was the little light known as the 'corpse candle'. This light would travel the route to be taken by a funeral procession, from the house of the deceased to the future grave. Just how often this sight accurately predicted a death is uncertain, but it was a belief widely-held.

Naturally, a lot of folklore superstitions were connected to animals, but it is surprising how many of them feature foxes. To see a single fox in the morning was a good omen, but to see several at any time was not. The appearance of a whole litter of young foxes close to a farm or house was a terrible thing; death or awful trouble would soon follow. The unusual sight of a white fox, however, meant different things according to where one lived. In most of South Wales it was an omen of death, but one farmer in Brecon insisted that if a white fox were seen near a large farm, it meant that an excellent harvest could be expected there. In Mid-Wales it foretold a good marriage, or the birth of a child who would be lucky in everything he did.

Finally, keeping the best superstition for last... my favourite snippet of folklore features one of my favourite places; Capel y Ffin, where it is said that the 'foolish people' who lived there once went out with bags to catch the moon, because they believed it was a cheese.

Bibliography and Further Reading

Carrington, H.,	True Ghost Stories,	J.S. Ogilvie 1915
Chadwick, E.,	To Defy a King,	Sphere 2011
Chadwick, E.,	The Scarlet Lion,	Sphere 2007
Chatwin, B.,	On The Black Hill,	Vintage Classics 1998
Clare, H.,	Running For The Hills.	John Murray 2006
CRiC,	A History of Llangattock,	2011
CRiC,	A Tour of the Holy Valley,	2018
Davis, P.,	Sacred Springs,	Blorenge Books 2003
De Bertouch, B,	The Life of Father Ignatius,	Methuen & Co. 1904
Erskine, B.,	Lady of Hay,	Harper Collins 2011
Fairs, G.L.,	A History of The Hay,	Phillimore 1972
Fox, C.,	South Wales & Monmouthshire,	HMSO 1955
Grinsell, L.V.,	Folklore of Prehistoric Sites,	David & Charles 1976
Hando F.J.,	Rambles in Gwent,	R.H. Johns, Newport 1924
Hando F.J.,	The Pleasant Land of Gwent,	R.H. Johns, Newport 1944
Hando F.J.,	Journeys in Gwent,	R.H. Johns, Newport 1951
Hando F.J.,	Monmouthshire Sketch Book,	R.H. Johns, Newport 1954
Hando F.J.,	Out and About in Monmouthshire,	R.H. Johns, Newport 1958
Haslam, R.,	Powys,	Penguin 1979
Leather, E.M.,	The Folk-lore of Herefordshire,	Logaston Press 2018
MacCarthy, F.,	Eric Gill,	Faber & Faber 1990
Nicholas, A.,	Supernatural Wales,	Amberley Publishing 2013
Palmer, R.,	Herefordshire Folklore,	Logaston Press 2009
Penman, S.,	Here Be Dragons,	Penguin 1991
Phelps. D.,	Haunted Hereford,	The History Press 2011
Plaidy, J.,	The Prince Of Darkness,	Arrow 2007
Plomer, W, (ed,)	Kilvert's Diary 1870-1879,	Guild Publishing 1986
Pugh, J.,	Welsh Witches & Warlocks,	Gwasg Carreg Gwalch 1987
Rieu, E.V.,	Gerald of Wales,	Penguin 1978
Sheers, O.,	Resistance,	Faber & Faber 2011
Sinclair, I.,	Landor's Tower,	Granta Books 2002
Underwood, P.,	Ghosts of Wales,	Corgi 1978
Williams, R.,	People of the Black Mountains,	Chatto & Windus 1989

Accommodation

Brecon

Black Mountain Lodge
Three Cocks
Brecon
T: 01497 847897
E: lodge@blackmountain.co.uk

Felin Fach Griffin
Brecon HR3 0UB
T: 01874 620111
E: Laura@eatdrinksleep.ltd.uk

Peterstone Court
Llanhamlach
Brecon LD3 7YB
T: 01874 665387
E: enquiries@peterstone-court.com

Capel y Ffin

The Grange Guest House,
Capel y Ffin NP7 7NP
T: 01873 890215
E: grangetrekking.guesthouse@gmail.com
W: www.grangetrekking-wales.co.uk

Clyro

Baskerville Hall Hotel
Clyro Court
Clyro HR3 5LE
T: 01497 820033
W: www.baskervillehall.co.uk

Pottery Cottage
Clyro HR3 5SB
T: 01497 822931
E: doblemdesign@gmail.com
W: www.potterycottageclyro.com

Crickhowell

Gliffaes Country House Hotel
Gliffaes
Crickhowell NP8 1RH
T: 01874 730371
E: calls@gliffaeshotel.com

Llangattock Park House
Crickhowell NP8 1LQ
T: 01873 810119 / 07988579124
E: booking@llangattockparkhouse.co.uk

The Bear Hotel
High St
Crickhowell NP8 1BW
T: 01873 810408
E: bearhotel@aol.com

The Dragon Inn
47 High Street
Crickhowell NP8 1BE
T: 01873 810362
E: enquiry@dragoninncrickhowell.com

The Kestrel Inn
Brecon Road
Crickhowell NP8 1SB
T: 01874 731044
E: richard@thekestrelinn.com

The Manor Hotel
Brecon Road
Crickhowell NP7 1SE
T: 01873 810212
E: info@manorhotel.co.uk

The Old Rectory Hotel
Llangattock,
Crickhowell NP8 1PH
T: 01873 810373
E: oldrectoryhotel@live.com
W: www.rectoryhotel.co.uk

The Red Lion
Dyffryn Road
Llangynidr, Crickhowell NP8 1NT
T: 01874 730223

Ty Croeso
The Dardy
Llangattock, Crickhowell NP8 1PU
T: 01873 810573
E: tycroeso@gmail.com

Usk Cottage Bed & Breakfast
Coed Yr Ynys Road
Llangynidr, Crickhowell NP8 1NA
T: 01874 730683
E: helen.griffey@btinternet.com

Glasbury

Foyles of Glasbury
Glasbury-on-Wye HR3 5LH
T: 01497 847550
W: www.foylesofglasbury.com

The Harp Inn
Glasbury-on-Wye HR3 5NR
T: 01497 847373
W: www.theharpinn.co.uk

Hay-on-Wye

Hay-on-Wye TIC
Oxford Road
Hay-on-Wye HR3 SDG
T: 01497 820144
E: post@hay-on-wye.co.uk

Hay Stables
Oxford Road
Hay-on-Wye HR3 5AJ
T: 01497 820008
W: www.haystables.co.uk

La Fosse Bed & Breakfast
Oxford Road
Hay-on-Wye HR3 5AJ
T: 01497 820613
W: www.lafosse.co.uk

Mulberry House Organic B&B
Gypsy Castle Lane
Hay-on-Wye HR3 5EG
T: 01497 821358
W: www.mulberrytree.biz

The Bridge Bed & Breakfast
4 Bridge Street
Hay-on-Wye HR3 5DE
T: 01497 822952
E: info@thebridgehay.co.uk

The Firs Guest House
Church Street
Hay-on-Wye HR3 5DQ
T: 01497 821800
E: thefirsathay@gmail.com
W: www.firs-hay,co,uk

The Globe at Hay
Broad Street
Hay-on-Wye HR3 5BG
T: 01497 821762
W: www.globeathay.org

The Old Black Lion
Lion Street
Hay-on-Wye HR3 5AD
T: 01497 820841
E: info@oldblacklion.co.uk
W: www.oldblacklion.co.uk

The Seven Stars
11 Broad Street
Hay-on-Wye HR3 5DB
T: 01497 820886
E: bookings@theseven-stars.co.uk
W: www.theseven-stars.co.uk

The Start
Hay-on-Wye HR3 5RS
T: 01497 821391
W: www.thestart.net

Tomatitos
38 Lion Street
Hay-on-Wye HR3 5AA
T: 01497 820772
W: www.haytomatitos.co.uk

Llanthony

Llanthony Priory
Llanthony
Abergavenny NP7 7NN
T: 01873 890487
W: www.llanthonyprioryhotel.co.uk

Accommodation – Self-Catering

Glasbury

Quarry Cottage
Ffynnngynydd
Glasbury-on-Wye HR3 5LU
T: 07752 938029
E: quarrycottage@googlemail.com

Curlew Cottage
Heol-y-Gaer
Glasbury-on-Wye HR3 5NX
T: 01497 847422 07976308226
E: angiecwhitlock@gmail.com

Hay-on-Wye

1 Sackville, via St Mary's Road
Hay-on-Wye HR3 5EF
T: 01497 821826
W: www.1sackville.com

A Sleep in Hay
27 Castle Street
Hay-on-Wye HR3 5DF
T: 07989 575131
W: www.asleepinhay.com

Brocklebank Cottage
Chancery Lane
Hay-on-Wye HR3 5BL
T: 07825 111279
E: info@brocklebankcottage.com
W: www.brocklebankcottage.com

Cariad Cottage
16 Bear Street
Hay-on-Wye HR3 5AN
T: 07973 409901
W: www.hayonwyeaccommodation.com

Chancery Cottage
17 Chancery Lane
Hay-on-Wye HR3 5BL
T: 07771 524940
W: www.chancerycottage.co.uk

Clay Cottage
Hay-on-Wye HR3 5RH
T: 07779 657515
W: www.clay-cottage.co.uk

Hay Cheese Market
Market Street
Hay-on-Wye HR3 5AF
T: 01497 821403
W: www.haycheesemarket.org

Hay Retreats
24-26 Millbank & 12 Market Street
Hay-on-Wye
T: 07908 978477
W: www.hayretreats.com

Lion Street Cottage
12a Lion Street
Hay-on-Wye HR3 5DB
W: www.lionstreetcottage.com

Smallbrook Cottage
Smallbrook Terrace
Hay-on-Wye HR3 5AX
T: 01497 821762
E: mandy@smallbrookcottage.co.uk
W: www.smallbrookcottage.co.uk

Llanigon

The Lea
Llanigon HR3 5QA
T: 01497 820283
E: lutherandnita@gmail.com
W: www.thelea.net

The Meeting House
Penyrwrlodd
Llanigon HR3 5PX
T: 01497 821822
E: anna.julian@gmail.com
W: www.hayonewyeholiday.co.uk